1947 Reading

Iowa Branch W.S.W.S.

A NEGRO'S FAITH IN AMERICA

THE MACMILLAN COMPANY
NEW YORK · BOSTON · CHICAGO · DALLAS
ATLANTA · SAN FRANCISCO

MACMILLAN AND CO., Limited
LONDON · BOMBAY · CALCUTTA · MADRAS
MELBOURNE

THE MACMILLAN COMPANY
OF CANADA, Limited
TORONTO

A NEGRO'S FAITH IN AMERICA

BY

Spencer Logan

NEW YORK · 1946

THE MACMILLAN COMPANY

325.26
L83

16826

Preface

THIS book is about my belief in America and my faith in the willingness of her people to accept the moral obligations of a democratic way of life. I hold to the view that the spirit of most of my fellow citizens is good, and will rise, in any great crisis, above the selfish desires of the few.

Because of my faith in the American people, I believe that they will come to an understanding of one another, if they are encouraged to do so, and if they are kept informed by their leaders of the importance of the American way of life. Those in our midst who are strong can show us how to help one another. The weak and the helpless will always be a reminder of how far we are from our ideal.

I believe that America will always rely on the wisdom of all the people to decide vital issues. The Negro representing some of the people wants to give of his best to the future of his country and to add his racial gifts of human understanding, patience, and industry to the welfare of all. America has long accepted these gifts as a matter of course. I believe that now she is groping for some way to give to the Negro greater economic security and his just rights as a citizen.

What I have to say is my personal opinion. It may well be misunderstood by some whites and even more by some members of my own race. As a Negro, my pride of race is strong; but this pride is tempered by the knowledge that in America my race is on the spot. To go forward the Negro people must become self-critical.

I have tried to face without shame the things we Negroes must do to prepare ourselves for a better postwar world. I have not hesitated also to say that the white race in America must arouse its sleeping conscience and stretch forth willing hands to grasp what may be its last opportunity to create a better world for all of us, regardless of race or creed.

This book is dedicated to all those who by their efforts are trying to find the way to a better racial understanding.

SPENCER LOGAN

OKINAWA, September, 1945

Contents

★ 1 ★

I Am a Negro-American

I AM a Negro-American. All my life I have wanted to be an American.

When I was young, all the great men of America were heroes to me: I gave my allegiance to George Washington, Andrew Jackson, Abraham Lincoln, Thomas Edison, and many others without stopping to think whether they were white or black. My teachers seemed sincere in the examples of success which they placed before me, and at first I did not realize that their advice was not for me. This I was to learn very slowly.

Yet in many ways I have been fortunate. In Elizabeth, New Jersey, where I grew up, I was elected president of my sophomore class in high school, although most of my classmates were white. As a member of the track team, I won and lost relay races with white teammates.

As an editor of the school paper, I had a white staff working with me; and I still recall with pride and pleasure the conferences at which we all, white and black, shaped editorial policies. I also remember the surprise with which I received news of my election to the Hi-Y Club, a high-school organization which was connected with the activities

1

of the Y.M.C.A. I was the first Negro in our school honored by membership, and my only regret was that I could not afford to buy a Hi-Y pin. Through the Y.M.C.A. I attended Older Boys' Conferences which were interracial.

Outside my school life I had the use of supervised playgrounds, and enjoyed plenty of baseball and football. In play, whether supervised or not, my friends were white and colored. Our neighborhood teams would travel to other parts of the city to play football or baseball. The team with the highest morale and best spirit of cooperation that I ever knew included Italian, Dutch, German, Irish, Negro, Polish, and Jewish boys. As a Boy Scout, I went to camps where whites and Negroes played and ate together. We took hikes and studied trail finding and map reading as a united group. There was never more than the ordinary friction which exists between teen-age boys.

But as I grew older I found it more and more difficult to forget for any length of time that I was a Negro. Once, having earned some extra money scrubbing floors in an office building, I took my mother into the ice-cream parlor on the main street of my town. I was the proudest boy in town that day; that is, until the counter girl came up and said, 'We can't serve you here!"

I started to speak, but my mother touched my hand. We left the store. My mother's head was high; so I lifted mine and said nothing.

While in high school I was selected by the faculty one morning to take charge of the assembly exercises for the day. It was the first time that a Negro had been so honored, but my pride in the occasion was short-lived. The speaker of the day, from a local bank, whom I introduced, began his remarks by telling a joke in which he blandly used the epithet of racial derogation, "nigger."

At another time our track team was honored with a banquet at a local hotel. The manager of the hotel objected when he saw Negro track men waiting in the lobby and attempted to separate them from their white teammates and have them wait in a back room. The rest of the team protested vigorously, and the track coach told the manager that he would not tolerate discrimination against any member of his team; but part of my pleasure in the event was spoiled.

After being graduated from high school I was anxious to attend college; but first I wanted to save up enough money to see me through the four years' course with what I could earn on the side. I secured employment with an ice-cream caterer in my home town. This Negro businessman not only taught me the rudiments of business but gave me many invaluable lessons in human relationships. He had one basic philosophy: "Whatever you do, do it just as well as you can."

In his relations with everyone he was straightforward and dignified, with a certain reserve which was characteristic of him. His customers were drawn from all walks of life, but they had one thing in common—an appreciation of his product and a respect for the man who made it. I know that on many occasions he sacrificed his profits in order to maintain the quality of his product. Often in midwinter the price of fresh strawberries was so high that he had hardly any margin of profit in making and selling his fresh strawberry ice cream.

After two years of hard work and self-denial I had saved a sum of money which seemed to me sufficient. One week before college opened, the bank in which I had deposited my money failed, and most of my savings were lost. With what I had left, I attended Rutgers University for one year. Then, short of funds, and handicapped by the depression, I gave up the idea of finishing college and spent the next two years in domestic service. At that time it was a choice between this kind of work and the National Youth Administration, and of the two the former seemed preferable to me. I had already noticed what seemed to me the effects of government paternalism on some of my friends.

In domestic work I learned patience and acquired a knowledge of the problems of domestic workers. It was impressed upon me that domestic workers were often fortunate in the relationships which they established with their white employers, but that in some instances, and particularly in periods of widespread unemployment, they were the prey of unscrupulous individuals who took advantage of their unprotected status to keep standards of work high and wages low.

My own situation was a happy one, and I had enough leisure to study and to participate in the activities of various organizations, particularly the National Association for the Advancement of Colored People. I was impressed by their effective action in many cases involving the rights of the Negro, but depressed by the fact that many members of my race who needed most what they had to offer were not drawn to the association. This may have been because a certain false air of refinement and culture pervaded the meetings; but more probably it was because the Negro masses themselves lacked initiative and social awareness. This is fortunately much less true today.

After about two years business conditions had improved, and I left domestic work, was married, and, in partnership with my brother-in-law, opened an ice-cream parlor in Plainfield, New Jersey.

A year or so later came an experience which taught me much, both about the white world and about my own relationship to it. We had accumulated a little capital and decided to open a branch store in a near-by suburban community. This I was to manage, leaving my partner in charge in Plainfield. I leased a good business location on the main street, purchased the necessary equipment and stock, and made plans for a gala opening. An inspector from the health department had already visited the premises and had assured me that all requirements had been fulfilled. It was a blow, therefore, when I went to the city hall to pick up my license, to be informed that my application had been denied. No reason for the refusal was given.

Thinking that the delay was only temporary, but concerned about the financial investment we had already made, I consulted a good lawyer. He investigated the matter and expressed the opinion that it was a matter of racial discrimination, but that this would be hard to prove; the case could be taken to court, but there was no guarantee that the court would force the town to issue the license to operate the store. I also learned from Negro friends in the community that some of the white businessmen objected to a Negro's opening a business on the main street of their town.

My lawyer, who had already advised me to withdraw and to accept the financial loss involved, appeared once before the city council but obtained only a promise of reconsideration. The matter dragged along for about two months. Finally, the council announced that it would not grant my license. The reason it gave was that it might later want to widen the street at the point where my store was located.

I was faced with what seemed to me to be a major decision. The investment already made was not so great as to affect us seriously, but the principle seemed to me a very important one indeed. It was obvious that the city fathers were using a technicality to prevent me from opening a store on the main street. My lawyer had already been told informally that if I would consent to move my equipment and stock to a store in a less desirable part of town there would be no difficulty about a license.

Obviously the city council could use legal technicalities indefinitely, which, in all probability, the courts would sustain against me should I have recourse to them. Before I abandoned my project, however, I wanted to be certain that the city council's action really represented the sentiment of the town, and that there was nothing I could do to awaken the community to what I considered an injustice.

Without consulting my lawyer, I decided to see what I could do. I first got in touch with individuals who were active in the local Negro church and through them gained the support of influential white Christians. The more reactions I had from white members of the community, the more I felt that the majority were on my side, and that the members of the city council were misjudging the sentiment of the town as a whole. This gave me sufficient self-assurance to enable me to visit each member separately and to present to him in person my side of the picture and the important issues which, I felt were involved. I found each councilman, when approached in this way, courteous and reasonable and, what was even more important, ready as an individual to admit the justice of my case.

The result was that I appeared at the next meeting of the city council, and the license was granted. Since then I have been convinced that many of the manifestations of race prejudice which we as Negroes experience would be greatly reduced if only those who yield to it could be brought face to face with the effects of this prejudice upon the human beings concerned.

Looking back from the vantage point of my early thirties, I have a greater understanding of the character of my grandfather and his influence on me when I was a child. All his life, he had lowly jobs; but he seemed to me in my youth to be the wisest man I knew. Although he had had no formal education whatsoever, he always sought knowledge; and it was with him that I first explored New York's museums, zoological parks, and scientific exhibitions. Once, at a marine exhibition, his knowledge of ships left me wide-eyed with amazement.

He often said he learned from people; and whenever he comes into my mind's eye, I see him talking to someone. His acquaintances were from all walks of life, both black and white. So he learned from people, and his knowledge covered a wide range of human relations. On one occasion he said at a Negro mass meeting which was stirring race feeling to a fever pitch:

"White people are human, the same as we are. Some of them are selfish and greedy; others are big in spirit. Some of them expect something for nothing, just as some Negroes expect to get democracy for the asking. They are not better or worse than we are. And, what is more important, we and they worship the same God."

I have seen white men, too, who learned from people. They were wise and educated without formal learning. I wish America could appreciate such men, and I wish America could forget that some of them are white and some are black.

My grandfather was a devout Christian and was proud of his position as a patriarch of our church; but he was never a strait-laced reformer. He often said that there were just as many "cussed" people in the church as out of it. His great faith in Christianity as the best fusion point of all racial differences impressed me, and today forms one basis of my hope for a better America, in which races will understand one another. The basic teachings of Christianity make a mockery of all those who proclaim their superiority because of race.

I have given this brief statement of my background and experiences before entering the Army so that the reader may judge the point of view from which I write. If America does not like all that I have to say, it is perhaps in part the result of what she has given me. At times I am bitter and speak rashly and in anger. Again, I may be foolish, forgetful of my grave obligation to my fellow men, whether black or white. My country has sometimes deprived me of full participation in the life around me. Jobs have been denied me because of my race, and I have felt the sting of being forced to live in undesirable areas. When a scapegoat was wanted, that scapegoat has often been my people.

In spite of all this I believe in America. My people believe in America. All the subtle persecution in the world cannot take our faith away from us. I rely on that faith.

I am proud that my people have instinctively rallied around the banner of democracy gone to war. Girded for battle with half-truths, aware of the hypocrisy of Americans who expected us to die even though they were unwilling to grant us a full share of life, we have been growing up overnight. The Negro of tomorrow will want to share in the benefits of society, whether this society encompasses the world or stays within the confines of the American scene.

Our growing pains are in evidence. I know that the Negro will not for long be satisfied with a half-crust. Nor will he necessarily shout his desire from the housetop. America must look into the hearts of my people and understand.

I am an American. I want to be treated as an American. If I wash dishes, give me the rights you extend to a white dishwasher. If I scrub floors, give me the right to walk among you as a man when my work is done. If I dig ditches, allow me to earn as much as a white man doing the same work. If I am a chef whose delicacies please your palate, do not picture me as a black grinning lackey. If I can set your heart to singing with rhythmic poetry or great music, respect me as a human being at the same time. If I have a touch of genius that enables me to delve into the great unknown of science and nature and to discover secrets and truths which mankind can use to create a better living for all—accept the rewards as the offering of a fellow citizen. And let your thanks be expressed in your greater feeling of a common humanity with all people.

I, too, am at fault. Many times I have failed. I have accepted many easy ways. I know that my people are divided among themselves, and that they are not equally ready to accept the responsibilities of full citizenship. But there is too much good and too much bad in all Americans, regardless of their color, for any American to expect perfection from the rest. Unless we are accepted, each one of us, for what we can give and what we can do, democracy, which is founded on the rights and obligations of the individual, can never maintain its high place in the hearts of mankind.

Our country, perhaps the most advanced democracy in the world, is still in the process of development. The democracy we seek has not yet been realized in the lives of all the people of the white race, and possibly never will be, for all the people are not capable of understanding and appreciating democracy.

Negro America is asking for democracy as a Negro. That in itself is un-American since it is class pleading, for true democracy should have the well-being of each and every citizen at heart. "The aim of a Christian social order," said William Temple, the late Archbishop of Canterbury, "is the fullest possible development of individual personality in the widest and deepest possible fellowship."

The belief of the Negro in America is a great challenge to America. It is a test of how much or how little faith white America has in democracy. It is not a challenge which can be met by a bank note or the passage of a series of unenforceable laws. It is a challenge to each American which can be answered only by a new conception of Negro and white relationship. This conception must find its ultimate expression in the development of an understanding between individuals, regardless of race, creed, or color—for that is democracy.

★ 2 ★

Leaderless

HAVE the Negro people developed a man or group of men who can lead them and speak for them in the postwar era which lies just ahead?

The mere development of creative talent, no matter how great, does not, it seems to me, necessarily fit an individual for leadership. Many of the Negroes who are prominent because of their creative talents or their success as interpretive artists are not in the real sense leaders of the Negro people.

These men and women, including some of the most eminent and distinguished members of the Negro race, are obviously moved by the artist's desire to give of himself to humanity. But I wonder if it is not also from a sense of social frustration—which even with their gifts they cannot shake off—that some of them have attempted a leadership for which they are not emotionally fitted. Between these individuals and the Negro masses which they represent, there is a spiritual gulf. These gifted men and women are not of the people. Their policy of stressing social equality rather than the building of a strong Negro society is indicative of their desire to get away from being Negroes. Any kind of leadership that arises from such frustration is not of the Negro people as I know them.

Another group which has assumed a position of leadership in the Negro race is that of the Negro intellectual idealists. Yet it is evident that the aims and needs of the Negro people cannot be set forth by this group of individuals alone. For they are too often theorists and agitators, even at a time like the present when the bulk of the Negro race feels that an immediate and practical means must be found for establishing working relations with the white race on a common front against the forces which are still threatening our democracy.

To my knowledge, none of these idealists has as yet displayed the vision of Gandhi, who wears a loincloth and eats the simplest of foods so as to be as near as possible, even in a physical sense, to the people he wishes to lead. As yet they have not shown even the simple greatness of Booker T. Washington, who told of his ability to dust a room so thoroughly that it pleased the meticulous lady of the house. It is not that one expects leaders to wear the dungarees of the migrant workers or eat grease-laden Southern food; it is only that they must find within themselves a chord responsive to the hearts of the Negro people.

During the past few years a new technique of leadership has been developed by certain Negroes who pose as spiritual leaders. These individuals seek to influence the urban Negro masses by appealing first of all to their religious instincts, since the Negro is deeply conscious of God. Having thus gained the confidence of his followers, by a show of great spiritual fervor, this new kind of Messiah attempts to go further. In contrast to the old type of Negro preacher, he soon abandons the field of purely spiritual values and endeavors to influence the social and economic views of his followers.

Leaders of this type have been deeply impressed by the success of communism in withstanding the onslaught of the German Army and turning the tables on the enemy. They feel that the Communist party must be given full credit for the results which have been achieved. Their admiration of Russian military success extends to the social accomplishments of the Soviet government and has led these supposedly spiritual leaders to adopt methods and attitudes characteristic of Communist organizations everywhere. They have, for instance, used the threat of force in an effort to obtain legislation guaranteeing economic rights. They have called belligerent mass meetings in which all the tried and tested techniques for arousing mob hysteria have been utilized. The speakers at these meetings talk in glittering generalities. All the superficial and age-old imperfections of democracy are criticized, with no attempt to point out the progress that has been achieved in alleviating its injustices.

These leaders cry out for new laws which, they tell the people, will guarantee all the benefits of society which are now denied to them. They speak rashly of creating in a day a world of justice and fair play. In their impatience, they mislead their followers into believing, after each small and insignificant victory is won, that greater agitation and sharper threats of force will produce proportionate victories instead of the inevitable reaction.

This senseless belligerency created the atmosphere for the recent rioting in New York City, where a Negro element of Harlem went berserk, destroying property and injuring innocent bystanders. The rioting could not be explained directly in terms of hunger for food. It could be attributed, however, to the constant agitation carried on by Negro leaders for the letter of democracy.

The ideal of democracy demanded by many Negro leaders is in harmony with the theory of democracy for all; but it ignores reality. The reality of the situation is that many Negro and white people are not ready to assume the responsibility of citizenship in a progressive modern state. One of the first needs of the mass Negro is a better understanding of the present-day crisis in American life and a recognition of his own responsibility in relation to it.

The extent to which Negro leadership has drifted from a program in harmony with the needs of the Negro in this crisis is indicated by certain aspects of the Negro press. Negro editors, aware of the inconsistency between the ideal of democracy as advocated by the Negro leaders and the discrimination and injustice endured by the average Negro, have attempted to emphasize the discrepancy by resorting to a type of headline which stresses the basic defects of Negro-white relationship: "White Policeman Shoots Negro Boy"—"White Man Slays Negro Sweetheart"—"Negro Youth Denied Entrance to White College."

These editors will say that, by political agitation, social and economic equality can be gained. Yet the feeling lingers in the hearts of many responsible Negroes that the problem presented has bread-and-butter roots, and that agitation yields at best only a few jobs.

The attainments of many Negro leaders of all types place them in the situation where they are lionized by certain groups of whites and given a taste of social acceptance. To them agitation for social equality becomes more important than it is either to the substantial middle-class Negro or to the many Negroes whose needs are still primarily in terms of bread and shelter. Such leaders enjoy the honor of their positions but do not share the everyday problems of their followers. Yet they are supported either by contributions from these followers or by jobs given them because they are supposed to represent their race.

Dr. George Washington Carver was a leader of quite a different sort. He avoided the many pitfalls of the Negro publicists. He developed his talent to the utmost, then gave freely of his wizardry to all people. He earned the gratitude and respect of white people. Dr. Carver set the highest possible standard for good race relationship, for he, as a Negro, achieved and practiced a concept of democracy which was in harmony with its greatest social and spiritual possibilities. Dr. Carver often said that he gave so freely of his talent because it was given to him by God. He subordinated his racial instincts to the good of democracy, and he believed that by dedicating his energies to the well-being of all mankind he would best serve his race. Dr. Carver more than any other Negro has set an example for Negro leadership of the future.

Since the advantages of a democratic society, particularly that of social equality, have become more and more desirable to many leaders as a result of their academic accomplishments and cultural attainments, they refuse to recognize in asking for these advantages that certain ones can be attained only through a process of evolution on the part of both the colored and white races. Moreover, the Negro leaders in question have neglected to impress their followers with the necessity of learning a trade through which they may contribute to the welfare of society. For this reason the Negro masses have developed an ineffectual attitude. They expect to receive the looked-for rewards without making the effort to prepare themselves to fill efficiently any specific jobs. This lack of training on the part of the Negro masses has disturbed many Northern Negro agitators; yet they have hesitated to admit the condition, for to do so would take the mantle of Negro leadership from their shoulders and place it upon those of the Southern Negro educators, who have consistently stressed a more practical approach to the Negro's economic welfare.

In a public debate which I heard over the radio, a Northern Negro leader was discussing with a white liberal some of the causes of discrimination. Discussing the economic aspects of this problem, the liberal pointed out that the South had been exploited by the North, with the result that the jobs which were available were hoarded by the whites and that the Negro workers had to take the leavings.

With realism and without personal bias the white speaker admitted, when challenged, that majority groups take advantage of their position and numerical superiority whenever economic conditions are such as to threaten their existence. "Is that right and ethical?" the Negro leader demanded. "It isn't right," said the white speaker, "but that's the way it is."

The Negro began at once to discuss heatedly ethical values and concepts of justice. His discussion was not an example of clear objective thinking but reflected instead his own personal sense of wrong and indignation.

Negro leaders must begin to study out realistic and practical solutions to the problems of their people. It is not enough for them to realize that something is wrong. They must evolve an answer to the problems at hand in terms of the human factors involved. For instance, in the matter of gainful employment many thousands of Negro workers, because of the influx of white workers into war industries, obtained jobs in non-essential industries and business enterprises. Negro economists are aware that these opportunities will not last; they know that as the veterans return, the Negro workers will be replaced by white workers. But analysis is not enough. They should devote all their energies and imagination to devising means whereby some, if not all, of these economic advances can be retained after the war. There is certainly plenty of leeway, under American labor laws and with the American instinct for fair play, for practical achievement in preparation for a greater degree of economic security for the Negro in the postwar world. But these plans must be kept out of the realm of what ought to be and must be concentrated on what can be done.

There are many Negro organizations which are dedicated to the task of obtaining social equality and a fuller share in democracy for the Negro by means of political pressure and court decisions. Such groups operate on the theory that the ideals upon which a government is founded can be enforced through the legal code of that country by test cases which establish definite precedents. They fight segregation by proving that it is legally wrong. They would wipe out lynchings by fining the county involved, or by making harsh prison sentences mandatory for anyone involved in them. They would loosen the economic noose about the neck of the Negro by the passage of more laws designed to make job discrimination illegal.

Negro leaders ruled by this thought pattern are in my opinion guilty, along with their white counterparts, of the gravest injustice to their cause if they attempt to gain by force of law alone the advantages of social equality from people who are not spiritually or morally prepared to grant it. They should realize that those who live by political agitation are by this very fact often handicapped as leaders; for a man who fights for the legal recognition of a principle may in the process lose sight of the human values involved.

Indeed, some of these leaders unconsciously assume a superior attitude toward the Negro masses. Some even become intellectual dilettantes. Their real trouble is often that, although they are prepared to serve their race and democracy, they are able to accomplish little. As a result, their pride is hurt, and their activities in the cause of social justice become primarily a means of satisfying their shattered self-esteem. They have, however, valuable attributes. They believe in the principles of democracy and in the dignity of the individual.

It must be admitted that wherever the Negro is politically strong some local advantages can be gained by the recourse-to-law theory. At best, however, such advantages are likely to be ephemeral since ground so gained shifts with changes in political fortune. The Negro must remember that all written law is subject to the greater unwritten law: the will of the people. It would be better for us if our leaders worked to create more good will and fewer laws.

Certain Negro leaders possessing more zeal than realism have propounded impressive but impractical plans for their people. These plans failed because with the existing political and economic circumstances surrounding the Negro they could not be realized.

There have been three plans of this sort for solving the Negro problem in America: the Back-to-Africa Movement of Marcus Garvey, the Sanhedrin Plan of Dr. Kelly Miller, and the Pan-African Congress of Dr. W. E. B. Du Bois. Each of these plans attracted a limited following, with the Back-to-Africa Movement proving the most popular among the masses.

The Back-to-Africa Movement led by Marcus Garvey aimed at establishing a civilized homeland for the Negro in Africa. To achieve this purpose, Garvey stimulated business enterprise among his followers and collected money for the dual purpose of financing his movement and his African settlement. The economic foundation he set up was not solid enough, however, to give stability to the movement. Without adequate funds the movement gradually dissipated itself. Garvey's conviction on mail-fraud charges added a stigma of moral delinquency to the plan and contributed to its failure. Its collapse left a scar of disillusionment in the hearts of thousands of Marcus Garvey's disciples who had followed him in the belief that if they could not live in harmony with white people in America, they could create a world of their own and find happiness in Africa.

Dr. Kelly Miller desired to sponsor a union of all Negro

organizations so that one central body, the Sanhedrin, would have the right to speak for the race on all major questions. But no one organization could speak for a race unless that organization had a definite program of action and a basic idea big enough to command the respect of the leaders of the smaller groups of Negroes throughout the country. Dissension followed, and the plan failed.

The Pan-African Congress developed from the scholarly interests and attainments of Dr. W. E. B. Du Bois. This plan aimed to develop a singleness of purpose among Negro people through conferences to stimulate cultural unity and the realization by the Negro that he was being defrauded of his birthright. The Pan-African Congress had no tangible objectives, however, and consequently appealed only to the intellectuals who already possessed common cultural aims and aspirations. The members of the Pan-African Congress, though conscious of their weakness, made demands upon Western culture which were either ignored, or tolerated only through the knowledge of their inability to make their demands effective. In fact, the Pan-African Congress did not even have the right to claim that it represented all the Negro people of the Western Hemisphere.

It is evident, however, that another force affected the potential success of these plans. This force was and is the instinctive impulse of any civilization to protect its own chances of survival. The proponents of all the plans overlooked this when they glibly announced their purpose to build up a unified world of Negro thought and ideas. Inevitably the fear instinct of white society was aroused when the efforts of Negro leaders to promote their plans resulted in the stirring up of racial distrust. Though these leaders were using the great privilege of freedom of expression, a privilege which is vital to Western civilization, they were intent upon setting up concepts and institutions which were alien and even unfriendly to this civilization. Dr. Du Bois through the Pan-African Congress wanted unity of Negro thought. Dr. Miller would have set up a central clearing house for Negro opinion which would in time have become autocratic in its operation. Marcus Garvey's plan, if successful, might have seriously affected the economy of certain parts of the country.

If, as it seems to me, the Negro race has not yet developed leaders who can be fully trusted to further the just ambitions of the race in the postwar world, from what group might such leaders be drawn? There is a large section of the Negro race which possesses what is the Negro's most valued quality —the simple capacity to get along with people and to give without expecting an immediate return. This is natural to the Negro, whose sense of giving is strongly developed. It is this trait of character which long made him the trusted friend of the plantation owner, in spite of the barriers of slavery.

I can think of many individual Negroes who have quietly and efficiently made important places for themselves, not because they were Negroes but because they were individuals with a contribution to make to American institutions. There is an increasing number of men and women in organized labor, industry, education, and even in our political life who fall within this category. Negroes who forge to the top in organized labor may perhaps be considered as representative of their own race in such organizations. But the same cannot be said of Dr. Henry A. Hill, who was recently named vice president of the National Atlantic Research Corporation, which is planning extensive research in postwar production of plastics, synthetic fibers, and surface coatings. His wife, Adelaide Cromwell, is a member of the faculty of Smith College. It is certain that William J. Anderson, who was recently elected to the State Legislature in Vermont from a predominantly white district, was chosen because of qualities which he could bring to his position as a leading businessman. In his maiden speech, Mr. Anderson declared: "You speak of freedom, gentlemen. I am the living example of freedom."

There are, in addition, many Negroes who never get into the news, and whose voices are never heard. They are thought of by some Americans as the racial exception, when actually they are the core and substance of the race. They are quiet, unassuming churchgoers. They fear God and have a deep sense of the will of God in their lives. They believe in America and the essential goodness of the white people of America.

These Negroes enjoy the confidence and good will of the people for whom they work, as well as of their co-workers. They rarely show anger except when someone insults them by talking down to them. Within the restrictions of their positions they have worked out a partial answer to the problems of racial discrimination. Organizations for race progress by means of agitation may attract them but will rarely hold their enthusiasm. They are not uninterested in race progress, but they feel almost instinctively that agitation is the wrong way for them.

It seems to me that this group is a spearhead which offers the greatest promise for an ultimate working relationship between the two races in America. The respect which they receive from their white colleagues is based on their achievements and a recognition of what they themselves can contribute as intelligent citizens. It is my belief that America as a whole must look to them and their methods for the solution of the Negro problem, and that from this group must eventually come the leadership to establish a new and finer basis of racial understanding.

Miscegenation from the Negro's Point of View

A NY discussion of a subject so heavy with emotion
must be undertaken with care, and in a spirit of forthright search for the truth.

One of the most humiliating experiences which the members of the Negro race suffer is the sense of debasement
when, as is the case in many areas, the sexual availability of
their women is never questioned. One Northern city I know
has a typical, overcrowded Negro area. Housing is inadequate. Crime is a way of life among some of the people of
this area, though many others are honest, hard-working men
and women who are trying to get by with a minimum of
trouble and a maximum of happiness under the circumstances. In the poorer areas of many American cities prostitu-
tion is a community problem, but upon this particular rubble
heap of social chaos there was piled an additional burden.
It was a practice (as I myself have observed) among white
men to come regularly and cruise slowly through this area
in their expensive automobiles. Any Negro girl on the street
was likely to be molested by such men. Not an occasional
car, but dozens of them cruised through the section nightly.
Decent Negro and white citizens demanded that these con-

ditions be changed. The police cooperated in the clean-up measures; in fact, they made it so unpleasant for white men they caught in the round-up that much of this traffic was stopped or driven underground.

The white men involved paid for their pleasures, and the Negro girls needed the money. But most Negro men deeply resented the situation. The white men were taking advantage of the Negroes' economic status and sense of social frustration. Poverty plus their feeling of social abjectness made the women susceptible to the advances of the white men.

Attempts to clean up such areas where miscegenation is rife usually result only in driving the antisocial elements underground. Any attempt to solve such a problem must be based on the recognition that poverty and social suppression make the weak individuals of all races susceptible to influences of demoralization.

This pattern of racial contact, based on sexual promiscuity, warps the mental attitude of many Americans, both white and Negro, toward a constructive solution of the race problem. In fact, too often, when confronted by interracial issues, white people will unconsciously betray their preoccupation with the thought of miscegenation by questioning the sincerity of those whites who show a humane attitude toward Negroes and, in extreme cases, by attempting to degrade all participants in interracial social contacts to the level of a lesser breed of humanity.

This preoccupation with miscegenation, which all too often becomes an obsession, strengthens the desire on the part of certain elements of the white population to segregate the Negro completely from white society. It leads in many cases to an unreasonable hatred of all Negroes. This hatred has some of its most obvious manifestations in the Southern states, where it adversely affects the economic position of the Negro and indirectly of the entire South. It is easy to understand that if a man builds a fence to keep someone confined he must stand guard around the fence, strengthening weak spots and checking all attempts to escape. This takes energy and time, and in a sense this is the plight of the white man in the South: his efforts to fence in and keep down the Negro have often limited his own economic opportunities.

One barrier to a closer drawing together of the white and Negro races in America has been the misconception on the part of many whites that the Negro race desires amalgamation. This issue is so weighted with emotion, hypocrisy, and suspicion that it has never been faced squarely. Speaking as a Negro, I know that most Negroes do not desire sexual relationships with white women. They have a sexual affinity with their own women which is to them more satisfying than any interracial sex expression. Negro men resent the mingling of white men and Negro women as much as white men fear miscegenation of white women and Negro men.

As for the old story that white women are not safe if the sexual desires of Negro men are not checked, it can bear investigation. If the number of cases of lynching is an indication of the frequency of attacks on white women by Negro men, then the matter is not serious. The existence of millions of mulatto Negroes resulting from the union of white men and Negro women bespeaks a worse record of forced relationships throughout American history. Women are subject to mistreatment at the hands of unbalanced men of all races. When the man is a Negro, he gets into the headlines; thousands of other miscreants do not.

In the beginning, under slavery, the Negro race was helpless. Admixture was forced on the Negro slaves at the whim of their white owners. After slavery was abolished, miscegenation was on a level of vice and crime, which in most instances took on the character of moral degradation on both sides. The amalgamation which occurred was bred of social injustice and wrong racial attitudes. When these forces are no longer at play, there will be less cause for fear on both sides.

The Negro is not interested in using social equality as a wedge to force himself into the home life of white America. He asks only that you do not intrude upon his hearthstone if you want the members of his race to honor yours. It is to gain the opportunity for better living that most Negroes want equality and not in order to be white or in order to associate sexually with members of the white race.

The problem as I see it must be approached from the point of view of individual evaluation, for it is not possible to say that all Negroes are on the same intellectual and social level. The Negro who has had the opportunity to gain a little self-knowledge does not want to become white. He is essentially Negro in spirit. Many who have had close contact with white people are not unduly impressed with the desirability of being white. One solution might be for thoughtful Americans to resolve that individual Negro citizens who prove themselves worthy will be given every opportunity to live their lives to the fullest in America.

Indeed, there is a strong likelihood that unless some definite step is taken to open fully the doors of economic and cultural opportunity to those Negroes who are prepared to enter them, they will lose faith and will become a liability to American life instead of a productive asset. If democracy is to survive it must provide the individual with the opportunity for self-expression in satisfying his economic needs, social desires, and cultural aspirations in accordance with his abilities.

Some whites will lag behind others in their understanding of the basic principles of a democratic society. Some Negroes will be unprepared for its full privileges. But we cannot afford to wait until all white people are prepared for democracy before granting it to the Negro. True democracy is not a way of life which gives to some men the right to do as they please and offers to others nothing but the possibility of a better existence some day in the future.

The Negro himself is constantly reminded that miscegenation has affected the development of his race. For the complexion of the Negro in America varies from white to very black. With these color variations there are also differences of facial structure and hair texture. Aside from their color many Negroes are comely by the best Mediterranean, Asiatic, or even Nordic standards. In some instances the combination of the Indian and Negro has produced a strong and virile type. Some of the variations in Negro types stem from their African background, for even on that continent there existed regional and tribal differences in the physical appearance of the Negro.

Variations in color were not important to the Negro in Africa; but in America his slave existence, with its horrible suppression of the opportunities for a normal life, created in him the need for any avenue of escape. Sexual relationships with whites offered one such means to the women of the race, and when children resulted from these relationships, they were often accorded opportunities and freedom of movement which were withheld from other slaves. Thus, the advantages of mixed blood took root in the Negro's mind and remained dominant for a period of about sixty years after the emancipation of the slave.

This feeling of superiority on the part of Negroes of mixed blood has been the cause of much friction and unhappiness within the Negro race. It was deplorable and in some ways pathetic. Light-complexioned Negroes were more easily hurt by the social ostracism and the economic discrimination that were imposed on them by whites. Influenced by their sense of superiority and urged on by their desire for greater security, these victims of miscegenation sought vainly to maintain a position in relation to their darker brothers which they thought white society accorded them.

In its heydey this cult of color had social clubs and religious groups in which a light complexion was essential to membership. Negro sororities became tinged with snobbishness. Cosmetic manufacturers reaped a golden harvest with bleach creams and ointments. Americans were presented with an interesting opportunity to observe a minority group which duplicated within its own ranks the injustices suffered by the entire group at the hands of a dominant society. With their sense of superiority the light-complexioned Negroes adopted social aggressiveness. They participated in interracial organizations, where they were the first to clamor for social equality. And to a degree they achieved this in their interracial gatherings.

Many of these light-complexioned Negroes were intelligent and acquired formal knowledge and basic skills in industrial production, which gave rise to the belief among the well-meaning white people who met them in interracial meetings that the mixed-blood Negro was more progressive and alert than other Negro types.

Some white people still try to draw a partial color line, and think that in doing so they are displaying a liberal spirit. They are not to be criticized for their views, but their attitude is grossly unfair to millions of Negroes who are not of mixed blood. It even affects adversely the economic situation of those Negroes who have dark skins. Recently a white plumbing establishment advertised for a light-complexioned plumber's helper. Advertisements of the same sort were common during the depression years, and many Northern housewives in that period sought light-colored servants instead of dark.

This attitude on the part of certain members of the white race is in marked contrast to that of the Negro race as a whole. To be sure, Negroes who are not of mixed blood, or who bear only slight evidences of white ancestry recognize the advantages which the lighter members of the race have in their dealings with whites; but they are also keenly aware of the disadvantages of mixed blood. It is generally recognized by Negroes that the lighter the color, the less stability of character and purpose, with, of course, notable exceptions.

The average colored man prefers a wife who is not too light, as he instinctively realizes that the stable characteristics essential in a good wife and mother are much less likely to be found in a light-colored girl.

The publication of a novel by George S. Schuyler, entitled "Black No More," has drawn the attention of American readers to the problem of the light-complexioned Negro. It has also brought home to many individuals in the Negro race the danger of allowing color variations to dominate their attitude toward their own race—a danger of which they have been rapidly becoming more aware.

Today any attempts on the part of whites to create a schism in the Negro race by appeals to groups of different color will, in my opinion, fail, even though such an appeal may represent a well-intentioned pattern of half-justice adopted by some cautious people. Such an approach will not be acceptable to the Negro since he is now united as never before and more alert than ever to any subterfuges which may attempt to separate a part of his people from the rest of his race.

★ 4 ★

The Harlems of America

THE American Negro has allowed one word and one area to become the symbol of Negro culture in the United States. The word is Harlem, and this word connotes to too many people throughout the world the pinnacle of Negro art and culture.

It is even more deplorable that a large majority of Americans draw their concept of the Negro race from the shallow depths of radio announcers who loudly proclaim: "The Crystal Ballroom presents Johnny Dude and his Hot Stompers." The music bursts into the loud-speakers of a million American homes, bringing with it the message of a Harlem's joy. A place exists where young people dance their cares away in wild abandon. A picture of dancing Negroes is drawn for America, of a Negro city where joy is supreme.

But the myth of the Harlems of America, those city areas in which all manner of frustrated Negroes live cooped up in tenements, must be exploded. Any picture of the "Crystal Ballroom" should include its immediate environment. Small dingy stores, vacant lots, saloons, and a general atmosphere of suppression surround it. Inside, is the fever heat of thoughtless youth indulging in exhibitionism. Girls, free of all social inhibitions, with skirts flying high are vainly trying to express their desire to be somebody.

But behind the Negro's laughter and dance mood is the haunting fear of insecurity and the ostracism of the unwanted. There is evidence of these fears, both real and imagined, which prompt the Negro to seek an escape from inner uncertainties in the emotional release of the dance, in the set expression of many jitterbugs midway through a dance frolic. The first novelty of the dance having worn off, the real significance of it all begins to show through their superficial laughter and to temper the wild abandon of their movements. Their expression becomes grim, and their movements lose their original flow and become static. Troubled in spirit but unaware of the source of their moodiness, the masses of Negroes, particularly in the urban areas, are not unlike their forebears in Africa who danced to ward off evil spirits. In America the evil spirits have taken the form of social injustice, race hatred, and economic discrimination.

This is the real background of the picture, but it does not come over the radio into a million American homes.

The white people who visit the Harlems of America often go away with a distorted picture of Negro life as one of too much pleasure amid poverty. They fail to realize that the Negro's instinct to survive forces him to rely heavily on the dance mood which is so strong in his people. And the areas consisting so largely of slums would be the deathtrap of the Negroes' people's destiny were it not for this ability to forget momentarily their problems and their surroundings. One condition creates the other and is dependent upon it. The Negro laughs to forget his plight, and his joy in laughter is the greater because of the nightmare of his environment.

The city Negro is surrounded by the best that civilization has created for the well-being and comfort of mankind, yet he is unable to enjoy it. His apartment may be steam-heated, but it is greatly overcrowded. Clothes are plentiful on the installment plan, with the bills rarely paid up. Education can be had; but there is no incentive to learn, for opportunities in skilled occupations are limited. Church life is abundant, but he often cannot share in it because he must work on Sundays in his bottom-of-the-ladder job. The Negro of the city is caught in the web of the struggle to survive at its worst.

Even the right to vote, though welcome, seems to be of little avail. The Negro's vote is too often nullified by the machinations of political bosses. Little wonder, then, that the average city Negro is close to the verge of violence even though he knows it may be self-destructive. Little wonder that the youth seeks forgetfulness in wild ecstatic dances, a casual studied indifference, or in the half-hearted adoption of all manner of radical philosophies. The Negro cannot be expected to develop a well balanced way of life upon the foundation of the social quicksand which underlies his city environment.

Where poverty exists there exists also a desire to escape. Unscrupulous white men have used this desire of the urban Negro to their own advantage, and with consequent disrepute to the Negro. Invariably gambling establishments, pleasure houses, night clubs, and taverns flourish in Negro areas. These are patronized by white people seeking a new thrill, and it is on this level that much of the contact between the two races occurs.

It is not uncommon to see whites who would not associate in their own homes with members of the Negro race mingling with Negroes in these places of entertainment. It might also be added that most of the Negroes who frequent such places would not be welcome in the better homes of their own race. So the worst in one race is exposed to the worst in another.

There are many other unwholesome and frustrating influences in the Negro life of big cities. Sometimes it seems as though a deliberate attempt is made to see that Negroes have access to plenty of liquor for forgetfulness. Shades of the Japanese selling opium to the Chinese! One thing which all Negro urban centers have in common is the excessive number of drinking establishments in comparison with dwelling units. In some areas of America's Harlems there are so many taverns that each half-block of people patronizes and adopts a place as its own, much as housewives adopt a corner grocery store.

Housing conditions in Negro areas, which have mushroomed out of the cities of America, are one of the heaviest crosses which the Negro has to bear. In exchange for the rent he pays, he gets less comfort than white Americans. Usually he is allowed to settle in a neighborhood only after it has degenerated—after white groups have abandoned it as too shabby, too unhealthy, too bleak, unbearable. Yet the Negro is expected to pay, and does pay, an equal if not higher rent for such homes, deteriorated though they are. And in these areas he is given very little civic protection.

As soon as Negro families move in, zoning laws seem to vanish. Slaughterhouses, garages, gas stations, reeking factories, ugly warehouses—these are the background, the inspiration of Negro childhood. Trucks can travel everywhere. There are few restrictions to safeguard the lives of children in the crowded streets. The previously mentioned assumption that a Negro area is necessarily a legitimate location for brothels, does not in any way help to make the conditions of Negro life more bearable. And low elements of the white population constantly come to the Negro areas in search of pleasure. Consequently, institutions of vice sponsored by white and black racketeers flourish.

And even where efforts have been made to better the living conditions of Negroes, such reform-in-a-fence cannot keep out the contagion of the slums. The model housing unit for Negroes put up in Newark, New Jersey, known as the Prudential Apartments, did not automatically wipe out the influence of the slums upon the tenants selected, since in the immediate vicinity of this model unit there are no fewer than a dozen saloons and liquor stores. Cleaning up a slum area is like cleaning a garment. One cannot rub out one spot without leaving a ring. The whole garment must be cleaned.

Housing conditions, which were bad enough before the war, are even worse at the present time. Despite the absence of many men who are still in the army, the population of these Negro urban areas has been constantly increasing. Many of the wives of men in the service have flocked to the cities to await their husbands' return. In addition, numbers of Southern Negroes were drawn to the cities by rumors of high pay in war industries. Also, many Southern Negroes who have long yearned for a change of scene now for the first time have enough money to finance a migration.

The result is that the Harlems of America are more crowded than ever before, with an ill assortment of Negro types. Illiterates from the South, doctors of philosophy from universities, criminals from the jails of America, law-abiding and God-fearing men and women from middle-class families, and jitterbugging youngsters are thrown together in such areas. Their cultural desires and economic aims vary, in spite of the fact that they suffer the effects of the same social, economic, and racial prejudices.

And the slightest improvement in the Negro's lot, inconsequential as it may be in relation to the need, must be won from many enemies, both within and without. The inner enemy is the Negro's own disunity, and the outer is the pressure of unscrupulous white forces which prey on him, and to whose advantage it is to foster his disunity.

During the recent civic furor for public housing financed by the Federal Government, a certain Negro community was about to get one of these units. The real estate interests, however, began to fight. One of the weapons used in their fight was said to be a nationally known organization for young people, which had a local Negro branch. Through white members on the board of directors of this branch, it was made known to Negro leaders of the community that important supporters of the organization did not like the idea of the Federal Housing Unit.

The Negro members of the organization took sides, some opposing the project because of long-standing friendships with the white members of the board, others because they feared the loss of financial assistance from local supporters of the organization. In fairness, it must be said, however, that many of the Negro dissenters honestly did not believe in Federal housing. Their objection was the same as that of many conservative whites, who shortsightedly claimed that Federal housing would place too much of a burden on local taxpayers. In any case, disunity was achieved, and the housing project wrecked. The suspicion has been growing among many younger Negroes that some, at least, of the welfare organizations with branches in Negro areas are used as pulse-tapping units by powerful forces to whose interest it is to keep the Negro divided and subservient.

It is regrettable that jealousies already existing in urban Negro communities make this disunity easier to achieve. One Negro minister conceived the plan of building a city-wide recreation center on a lot next to his church. He asked other Negro leaders in the community to join with him so that he could go to interested white people with a united backing. They refused, some out of jealousy because the building lot was not next to their property, others because of religious scruples—so they said; and because of lack of support the plan fell through.

It is amazing how many sharply divided groups there are in any Negro urban center, and how the life of the community is divided by these egocentric fragments. The pathetic effort of the Negro city masses to find social expression is indicated by the great variety of insignificant societies, clubs, and political organizations which abound, and which are aggressive, self-conscious, intent upon their own petty aims, and blind to the larger world of their common problems outside. These battling organizations, with their individual credos and fancy uniforms, drain the poverty-ridden people of such funds as there are in the community and prevent concerted race action.

In a small Northern community, the Negro citizens had for years tried to place one of their race on the Board of Education. The controversy extending over so long a time was seemingly ended when the white political elements in the town agreed to accept a Negro member. This was a great victory for the Negroes, and there was much rejoicing until it became necessary for the various organizations in the Negro community to come together upon a candidate; and then the fruits of the victory were lost. In the battle that ensued, no name could be agreed upon, and so no name could be submitted.

But how can the Negro be anything else than disunited? He has not yet recovered from two violent upheavals in his social existence—namely, emancipation, and the wholesale migrations from the South to the North—for neither of which he was prepared. This latter event, the removal of the Negro from a familiar environment, and his sudden urbanization under most unfavorable circumstances, has not helped in solving his already complex problems.

Many Negroes came to the North in search of happiness and greater economic freedom. Ignorantly they thought that by changing their immediate environment they could better their conditions and improve their opportunities. But in most cases an old devil was exchanged for a new one. Forced to live in segregated areas, the transplanted Negroes soon had more problems than, it seemed, could ever be solved.

In labor they have been used as strike breakers. In politics they have been influenced to vote for men who did not represent them. Some of the Negro leaders began to look on the political power of the Negro masses as a whip, which, if wielded cleverly, could force the granting of fundamental rights. But after a time even the most obtuse political leaders discovered that the rights they could get had a price. Negro leaders were forced to cooperate with politicians in order to bring out the vote. Often the policies of these white bosses were hardly complimentary to the intelligence of the Negro. For electioneering was conducted on a level of free dances, beer parties, and the granting of concessions to political favorites enabling them to operate gambling houses, speakeasies, and brothels outside of the law. It was this bargaining that paved the way for the vice and crime of our Northern Negro areas.

Economically depressed, lacking opportunity except for the most menial and lowest paid work, misled by bewildered, frustrated, and sometimes corrupt leaders, the Negro who has emigrated to the city has not been able to pick the good things from the bad in the complicated environment which surrounds him.

To compensate for his environment and lack of opportunity, he has too often developed the illusory life that is typical of the urban Negro, and that distinguishes him from his rural Southern brother. There is something pathetic in the vision of an eighteen-dollar-a-week porter spending half of his salary on Saturday to rent a tuxedo in order to mingle with other menial workers in rented suits at parties which aspire to imitate white social affairs. The lighter Negroes have in many instances become color-conscious and have refused to associate with their darker brothers and sisters. Edu-

cated Negroes have set up cults of the educated which are
as useless as any form of social snobbery.

In trying to escape the hardships of segregation and discrimination present-day Negroes find themselves living in a
world supercharged with a strained emotionalism. The fer-
vent and showy religious cults and fraternal practices that
abound in the many Harlems of America are symptomatic
of a suppressed emotion.

The giving of divine attributes to certain leaders by their
followers results from the desire of people for a closer relationship with an all-conquering force. Vainly they seek from
religion a solution to their material needs. One of these leaders is said to do much good. It is conceded that some of the
economic weaknesses of this leader's organization are overcome by his good-will policy; for all his emotionalism he
stresses honesty and work in his program. However, the
lasting power of a program based on this kind of man-
centered worship is questionable, because when the leader
dies his followers must lose heart.

The need of the Negro for religious expression is so deep
that it can be exploited with considerable profit by those
who have the technique of showmanship. No investment is
required, and if enough fervor is aroused the financial return
will be large. What is more unfortunate is that not only the
meager pennies of the followers are exploited, but their
deepest feelings as well.

In a neighborhood where most of the people were on relief
a "store-front" church was set up. The exploiters of this one-
night stand aroused the people to such a high emotional pitch

that the response of the congregation attracted the attention of radio promoters.

The religious fervor of the meeting was unusual in its deep sincerity. The services went on the radio. A small station featured the program, which in time was sponsored by the small merchants of the neighborhood. Those who profited most, however, were the purveyors of the palliative, the religious leaders themselves, who drove around in big cars and lived well on their financial returns. In the meantime the people whose sincerity made the church successful were still living in rotting tenements and were finding their only outlets in the hysteria aroused by these leaders.

Very natural is the attempt to forget, either through religion or through preoccupation with pleasure. To interpret the urgent need for religion and the cults and beliefs practiced with such emotional abandon as evidence of simple-mindedness or contentment, is certainly shortsighted. The Negro's religion is one long supplication for help against an environment that is overpoweringly against him.

The home life of the average Negro, especially in the city, has always existed under the threat of economic insecurity. More often than was healthy for him the Negro wage earner was unemployed. Negro women have been forced to go out to do domestic work, or cheap-paying factory work. In lives so circumscribed there was, as is usual for the very poor, no other enjoyment possible than sex expression; for long hours of work left little time for other types of relaxation. Sexual laxity and marital irregularity, as well as parental irresponsibility, especially where the fathers are concerned, have all contributed under urban conditions toward breaking down family unity, which was formerly one of the strongest factors of Negro life.

With both parents forced to work, children could not and did not receive proper guidance. Many drifted into criminal activities. This may be true of low-income white family life, but without the added burden of racial discrimination. As a result of the disintegration of the home much of the propaganda sent out to influence the American people to defend their homes and democracy left the average Negro untouched. Imagine the feeling that must have come over a Negro family living in a cold-water, one-room flat, when they heard a radio announcement on the need to buy bonds, so that American homes and families could be protected.

There are a number of other burdens, such as the high-cost weekly industrial insurance sold to the Negro people. And many petty criminals, like present-day carpetbaggers, fatten on the circumscribed Negro life. They have changed their dress, but their methods are the same. Instead of carpetbags they carry policy slips, small loan contracts and fancy-name cards for all manner of organizations. The policy gambling racket takes hundreds of thousands of dollars out of the meager earnings of the Negro workers. Millions of future man hours of work have been mortgaged to pay for goods that would never have been bought except for the bait of the installment plan. Playing on the gullibility and frustration of the newly urbanized Negroes, high-powered salesmen have stimulated the desire for luxuries in homes where simple necessities are grossly neglected.

Nor does the Negro see any ready means of escape from

his dilemma. Because of the discriminatory practices in industry toward the Negro worker from the beginning of his free life, he has little reason to develop pride in work. His position as an unskilled worker was not conducive to the development of greater training; and for the trained and skilled workers among the Negroes there are few opportunities anyway. Often highly skilled craft unions bar Negro workers from membership. As a result many Negroes develop a defeatist viewpoint as to the possibility of participating more fully in the economic life of our highly industrialized and mechanized society. They even fall back on the childish belief that the world owes them a living because their ancestors were enslaved instead of thinking in terms of what they can do despite their handicap to secure greater economic security for themselves and their families.

I have often felt that more Negroes could and should enter the field of retail business even though I know that many men with ideas and initiative have been unable to overcome the difficulties such ventures have to face. Whenever a progressive Negro attempts to go into business he is subjected to various forms of pressure. Sometimes a real estate clique of white businessmen will make it hard for him to rent a store in a good business location. Either a white competitor will suddenly turn up with a lease on the vacant store or else the rent will be scaled higher than the prospective businessman can assume. Very often lack of capital prevents the new Negro businessman from securing credit for himself from wholesalers and thus extending credit to his customers and competing with his white competitors for the patronage of the neighborhood. In addition the average Negro lacks experience in business and is averse to the idea of undertaking the economic risk involved in going into business for himself.

There are, however, two factors which may well serve to give greater economic stability to Negro businessmen in the near future. These are the war savings accumulated by many, which can be utilized as capital for small enterprises, and the growing race consciousness of the Negro masses. The latter factor will mean increased patronage and backing for young Negroes who are willing to venture forth in the business world.

It will be fortunate if more of the latent abilities of the Negro people can be channeled into the business world, for the race must begin to play a greater part in America's economic life. In the past the best brains of the race have been devoted largely to organizational work.

Walter White of the National Association for the Advancement of Colored People, for example, possesses unusual executive ability and the courage of his moral convictions. Mr. White expends his great talents in a magnificent effort to create a better world for Negro Americans through recourse to the courts and legislatures. One wonders what he might have achieved if his remarkable executive ability had been used in developing a Negro industry or business.

America must reorganize and revitalize her economic system after the war so that the maladjusted industrial workers of all races living in crowded city areas may have a better life.

Out of the ruins of war, England and Russia will build model cities, planned to promote the health and welfare of their residents. America, not having ruins to rebuild, will nevertheless have to keep pace if the cancerous growth of social unrest is to be avoided. It is quite natural that the urban dwellers of America should expect to get as much in the postwar world as those of Russia and Great Britain.

In addition, certain changes in our economic life will be a matter of national expediency. The war has disclosed the dangers of industrial planning which concentrates the factories of a nation in a few areas. Aside from its military disadvantages, such concentration creates an unbalanced economy with resulting insecurity for industrial workers. It is unlikely that the American people, now that the war is over, will long be willing to tolerate such a haphazard and insecure economic arrangement.

City dwellers in particular have been subject to periodic unemployment. Of recent years government and local relief has kept unrest in check. Tomorrow, relief checks may not suffice for this purpose. New enterprises in non-city areas must create opportunities for a more secure and a better life for a greater number of people. In this new scheme of things there must also be found a place for the unused and unhappy people of the Harlems of America.

Hopeful Portents

ANY consideration of Negro-white relations would be incomplete unless it set forth the progress which has already been made toward greater understanding and good will between races in the United States. The present situation despite the social and economic stresses which war has brought, contains many hopeful aspects as the result of the work now being done by groups and organizations in various parts of the United States. Some of these movements represent local experiments aimed at furthering more democratic racial attitudes, which if successful may well spread throughout the country; others are already national in scope.

America is a potential proving ground, and perhaps the finest, of the theory that all men have within themselves a mental and spiritual unity. All racial and minority groups in America must come to the realization that democracy demands an allegiance to the welfare of all, regardless of color or creed. But this realization cannot be achieved by the threat of legal punishment. The sounder approach in the long run is through the persuasive power of education, always the strongest weapon of an informed democracy.

Springfield, Massachusetts, in its program of education in

democratic citizenship has set a brilliant example for other cities to follow. Its educational plan advocates and practices "in all the schools a common philosophy of education based upon the ideal of living, learning, working and thinking together." Dr. John Granrud, the Superintendent of Schools, is the driving force behind this new approach to better citizenship. His patience, vision, and humanity are guiding the program of education for better citizenship through its early stages.

The application of the plan begins in the elementary schools and continues through the junior and senior high schools. It provides for extracurricular activities, adult education classes, employment bureaus, and enlightened public relations. Other phases of the plan are a policy of arriving at important administrative decisions through a consensus rather than through arbitrary judgments; the delegation of real responsibility to working committees and to responsible individuals; a policy of promotions for teachers on the basis of merit, without regard to race or to political or religious affiliations; and the stimulation of individual initiative on the part of teachers and students working toward the common good of all.

Even in the elementary school a democratic attitude is stressed. Children are taught to respect their playmates in school regardless of race or creed, and those of foreign-born parents with inherited prejudices are steered into a path of tolerance toward other minority groups. The children learn to like one another by working and playing together. Through projects, the elementary schools cultivate in them an appreciation of the arts and skills of other races. Above all, the children become conscious of their responsibility to be friendly and courteous toward all their fellow pupils.

In junior high schools the children are given practice in democratic methods through councils and committees elected by themselves which exercise initiative in planning school and classroom activities and in putting these plans into effect. They are made conscious of the responsibility of every American to be a good citizen. In this drive to create a concept of good citizenship they are taught to appreciate the contributions of all races and nationalities to America as a whole.

The senior high schools stress other avenues of approach to the problem. Democratic practices in school and classroom management are developed. Also the students are taught to be watchful of cliques based on prejudice, either racial or religious. Before they leave high school the realities of life in America have been presented to them, and they are then in a position to compare the realities with an ideal American way. A feature of the high-school program is the town meeting, which gives the students an opportunity to discuss issues in public and to develop habits of straight thinking.

The parents also receive attention, and are encouraged to attend adult education classes for better citizenship. Group discussion is a feature of these classes, which are planned particularly to prepare aliens for the privileges and duties of citizenship.

The job placement phase of the program aims to provide jobs for high-school graduates, to overcome racial or religious prejudices among employers, and to raise minority groups to levels of great economic security.

Publicity is given to the program by talks, radio broadcasts, and the press. The public is constantly reminded of the work which is being done and is kept informed of any new developments. The program also sponsors nonpartisan meetings, at which candidates for public office of all parties are invited to discussions of public interest.

Negroes are taking an active part in this program. They are serving as teachers in the public school system, some specializing in particular fields of education. By contributing to the common good in helping other minority groups along the road to better citizenship these Negro teachers symbolize what democracy can be at its best.

Negroes can vouch for a gradual decrease in evidences of racial prejudice in Springfield. Beyond a doubt the good that has been achieved and the examples set form a pattern worthy of study by other American communities.

In New York the All-Day Neighborhood Schools of the Public Education Association and the Board of Education are developing a new approach to the problems of the metropolitan child. Two schools, Public School 33 and Public School 194, are vitally concerned in this program which sponsors a longer school day with a supervised play program for the children. The schools also work closely with the parents and neighbors of the children.

In Public School 194, Adele Franklin, recent winner of the Edward Bernays $1,000 award for outstanding contribution to the cause of democracy in education, is instructor in charge of all-day school activities. As a teacher she has gone far in her efforts to help the Negro pupils who attend the school. Many had no knowledge whatsoever of the historical background of their race or its outstanding figures, because in their textbooks the Negro was either ignored or passed over with scant recognition. They knew nothing about the arts and crafts of the Negro cultures of Africa. For the most part the children had chosen heroes of their own race from the athletic field and the night club because they knew of no others from whom to draw inspiration.

Adele Franklin sensed this tragic situation, wanted to do something about it, and did. With great patience and tact she turned the eyes of the children toward themselves. They were taught to feel proud of their African heritage. At the end of one term's work the pupils gave a play with Africa as its setting. The costumes and scenery were made by the pupils with a minimum of assistance from the teachers, the children themselves visiting the libraries to check on details. Significantly the Negro children managed to convey some of the beauty and mystery of Africa in their play.

Miss Franklin and her assistants go even further in their efforts to help these bewildered children keep faith with themselves. They present to the children any material that can be found on the great civilizations of Africa, so that they may acquire an appreciation of their own heritage of heroes, organizers, statesmen, and scholars.

White children from Public School 33 visit the Negro children at Public School 194, and, despite some initial misgivings on both sides, the children are soon at home with one another. This contact in childhood by future citizens, in which both whites and Negroes learn that they can play and work together, is one of the best ways of developing a democratic approach to racial problems.

Two significant facts were brought out in this work: first,

that the Negro children, when given a basis for racial pride, could more successfully meet with white children on a basis of equality; secondly, that textbook material with which to work was woefully lacking. It is to America's shame that such a dearth of material on the Negro exists; but there is reason to believe that this lack may be corrected in the near future.

In Chicago on Monday, May 8, 1944, the American Council on Race Relations was organized and a five-point program was announced. This provides for:

1. The advancement of knowledge concerning race and race relations by the collection and analysis of records and by original research.
2. Assistance to local communities in organizing to meet their interracial problems where the existing program seems inadequate.
3. Cooperation with public and private agencies and individuals working in the interracial field by supplying needed information, by advice concerning procedures, and by the temporary loan of personnel.
4. Assistance in developing materials and programs for use in public schools and other educational institutions.
5. The dissemination of knowledge about racial groups to the public, through the radio, press, movies, and any other means of popular education.

If the fourth point in the program is successfully carried out, the Council should be able to supply the need for adequate textbooks of the All-Day Neighborhood Schools of New York City, the Springfield schools, and the courses in Negro history being given in some of the Chicago schools.

George S. Schuyler, associate editor of the Pittsburgh *Courier* and a well-known Negro journalist, has developed an approach to the problem of racial prejudice which shows his grasp of some of the basic maladjustments of the Negro, particularly in urban centers. This progressive editor has a keen sense of the emotional tensions of Negro life and the effect of these tensions on the Negro. The program of his "Association for Tolerance in America" shows an astute understanding of both Negro and white psychology. One phase of this program is directed, by the use of posters and the press, toward urging the Negro to promote better race relations by watching his conduct in public. "You are judged by your talk, looks, actions," he is advised. "Be neat, quiet, sober, clean, steady, thrifty, healthy, punctual, courteous, industrious."

Mr. Schuyler is interested in enabling the Negro to develop those qualities of character which will increase his acceptability to American society as a whole. He is endeavoring to free the Negro from many obvious personality faults and habits which cause whites with whom he comes in contact to think of him as unprepared for everyday social relationships. This is an approach to the problem which might well be emulated by other minority groups.

The magazine *Color,* published in Charleston, West Virginia, is blazing the trail with a new type of Negro journalism. Its editors stress the constructive phases of Negro life. Outstanding achievements by Negroes are commented upon and illustrated by pictures. Even though, in covering the entire interracial picture, many depressing facts are necessarily brought out, the general impression gained by the reader is that progress is being made, and that there is increasing hope for the future. *Color* reports news of interest to all Americans, but highlights that of special importance to the Negro. Its Negro readers, realizing that the magazine is quietly fostering good will among both races, and that it is working to develop the Negro's personality and to show him at his best, have rallied enthusiastically to its support.

In the South the Southern Regional Council—an interracial group composed for the most part of educators, ministers, liberals, and labor leaders—has adopted a seven-point program which is aimed at the development of better relations between whites and Negroes. Much of the value of its work lies in the stress it places upon the economic ills confronting the Negro worker. It aims to achieve employment of all persons on the basis of ability—including more colored policemen and firemen, equal treatment for all by police and the courts, abolition of the white primary, equalization of educational facilities and teachers' salaries, extension of publicly financed low-cost housing, and the promotion of publicly financed medical and dental treatment for all on an equal basis.

The right type of organization can be of great assistance to Negro workers in establishing direct contact between themselves and management and in bridging the gap between war and peacetime employment. The sort of movement which might well be extended is exemplified by the National Association of Negroes in American Industry. This association gives awards to employers for outstanding achievements in the use of Negro labor. It is made up entirely of Negroes, deals directly with employers, and does not have to rely on liberal white intermediaries; its effective methods should receive much wider publicity.

If the citizen, whether white or Negro, is to contribute his full share to the general well-being of America, he must be made to feel that the job he does is important, and that both government and society recognize this fact. Our government has long realized its obligation to the industrial workers of the country, but it has ignored other groups. Domestic workers, for example, have little or no protection and represent, in many respects, the stepchildren of American labor. This is due, in part, to the fact that domestic workers, isolated as they are from one another through the nature of their employment, have had less incentive and opportunity to organize effectively.

Just before the outbreak of the Second World War, certain subversive elements were fomenting ill will between Negro domestic workers and their employers. Their consciousness of economic insecurity as workers was played upon in order to increase interracial tension. That tension, if allowed to persist, could have far-reaching effects, as the home is a dangerous place for interracial misunderstanding to develop. Such a development can easily defeat educational plans and good-will programs.

After this war, many women will of necessity return to domestic work. They may do so with many misgivings. The old conditions, if allowed to continue, will revive past grievances and develop new friction between the two races. To avoid such repercussions the people of America should face the issue squarely. Plans should be formulated to foster greater pride and satisfaction in their jobs on the part of the workers and the acceptance of higher standards of work and pay by employers. Through government or other agencies adequate training should be made available to persons who wish to engage in domestic service. Established standards of skill and experience should be recognized in each community, both by employment agencies and by potential employers. In any case, experienced and skilled domestics should not be forced to compete with the inexperienced in a cutthroat labor market. After eliminating unsatisfactory employment practices, some method should be found of establishing group unemployment and pension plans, either independently or under an expansion of the Social Security Act. Such protection would go far toward helping to create an atmosphere of good will between the domestic employee and employer and would give a sense of security to domestic workers turned loose from the safe harbor of government-sponsored war industries.

The National Negro Urban League is another organization which has done much to further understanding between the races. In urban communities it·has cooperated with industry in ascertaining the ability of a given area to absorb available labor. It has often helped to successfully chart the course of race relations, especially in times of crisis. For the most part, its policy has been to cooperate closely with industry and with civic authorities. The organization, however, is sometimes ineffective in its methods of appeal for popular support.

One of the most encouraging aspects of interracialism in this country is the increasingly important role which the churches have played in promoting better race relations.

The Protestant churches, prompted and encouraged by the Federal Council of the Churches of Christ in America, have long been active in this field—through the education of their congregations in proper racial attitudes, and the organization of interracial groups. The Catholic Church, although much less active in such organized means of combating prejudice, probably has displayed in actual practice fewer evidences of racial discrimination, either among its clergy or among its congregations.

Since the basic tenets of Christianity are the same as those of a true democracy, it is to be hoped that the churches will continue their activities in this field, on an even broader scale. Certainly the militant and constructive attitude of the Federal Council is doubly important at this time and may well serve further to enlarge the scope of Protestant activities in combating race prejudice throughout the country.

One limitation which has unfortunately interfered with the effectiveness of the churches of America in serving as media for promoting better race relations is the fact that our religious life in the United States is still far from united. Sectarian differences divide the communities themselves; and, in addition, attitudes of racial superiority still exist in much of our practice of Christianity. Negroes and white people generally worship separately through their free choice; but more might be done within the various churches to further an attitude of racial understanding. For example, interracial programs in which Sunday-school groups would exchange visits might accomplish the same ends which are being sought in the more progressive educational programs.

Important as the work is which is already being done in

America, no one can deny that the results are still inadequate, and that we are not yet prepared to meet any serious crisis in race relations such as is very likely to arise as an aftermath of the war. The hysterical manifestations of the revived Ku Klux Klan following the First World War should be a warning to us all that a situation may develop at any time which could, temporarily at least, undo much of the good which has already been achieved.

It is most important that the majority of individual citizens in the United States adopt both in theory and in practice a tolerant and friendly attitude toward other races. Much can be done toward this end through channels already established; but it may well be possible to work out a program, sponsored either by the government or by some national organization, for the establishment in every community where racial problems exist of active groups which might, for want of a better name, be called Good Will Clinics.

Such clinics could be staffed by public-spirited individuals who could contribute some of their time as a form of public service, or better yet by a nucleus of trained and paid workers, assisted by volunteers. The clinics themselves could serve as a means of educating their communities in democratic racial attitudes through the organization of public meetings and discussion groups, and through the use of the local press and radio. They would be constantly on the alert for the detection of any racial tensions which might arise from time to time, so that an incipient crisis could be nipped in the bud. Anyone suffering from the effects of racial discrimination, whether social or economic, could reply on the clinics for assistance and advice. Frequent reports on the progress being made could be given to the public; and, if the organization were broad enough in scope, many problems could be worked out on a national basis. A policy of watchfulness is sounder than a policy of hindsight—in the past, America has been too much inclined to ignore the harmful practices of society until they have become acute.

If the people of America are to get along with one another, regardless of racial and religious differences, they must become more aware of the need of making their democratic principles a part of their everyday lives. No citizen should be allowed to fail in the realization of his own responsibility for the welfare of the whole, with stress upon mutual respect among all. America has learned the technique of selling the public almost anything. We have been taught lessons of health and cleanliness, have been influenced to spend or save money, and have been united for the purpose of waging war against a common enemy. Why cannot similar educational techniques be used against those attitudes on the part of many of our citizens which may well prove to be as destructive as any foreign foe could have been?

★ 6 ★

The Negro Soldier

THE figure of the Negro soldier looms large in any discussion of his race in America. His successful postwar adjustment is essential to a better race relationship, since he is almost certain to represent a pivotal group within his race. This adjustment must be based upon an understanding by Negroes and whites alike of certain changes in the outlook of the Negro soldier brought about by his experiences in the war.

Our policy of segregated training has brought to the soldier a fuller realization of his position as a Negro. Although the American pattern of racial discrimination has kept him conscious of his race, this consciousness has been heightened by his army experience; and he has come to realize that the race problem is an inevitable part of his life, even in a democracy at war.

I can still recall vividly an instance which occurred during my own basic training. We were scheduled one day to see a morale and orientation film. Some white troops were at a similar stage of training, and it was arranged that we see the film together. Companies of white and Negro troops approached the theater from opposite directions and were marched into the building. The white troops went to the right, the colored troops to the left. The lecture and the film were concerned with an analysis of the virtues of democracy as opposed to Fascism. The tolerance and equality which exist in a democracy were stressed, and Fascist inhumanity to minority groups was condemned. I suddenly became acutely conscious of the fact that we Negroes were being trained to defend democracy, but that even during this training we were segregated from the white troops. I emerged from the lecture with a depressing cynicism which stayed with me for several days. I talked with other Negro soldiers who had attended the lecture with me and found that those from the North had had the same reaction.Those from the South had been less conscious of the segregation, but had, instead, been very much surprised that the ideal of democracy expounded in the lecture even existed in America.

For the most part, the Negro soldier has been under the leadership of white commissioned officers. He would have a greater respect for Negro commissioned officers if he did not feel that they themselves, rightly or wrongly, were in most instances kept in subordinate positions on account of their superiors' distrust in their ability. Even where men of his race have achieved high rank and authority, he is inclined to accuse them of having done so through the use of an "Uncle Tom" approach.

This feeling has not helped those who are endeavoring to improve the Negro's morale, since it has served to strengthen his conviction that the segregated army units to which he belongs are stigmatized with the old racial inferiority. And conditions in Southern camps served only to aggravate the case. In morale and orientation classes he listened to lectures on the ideals of democracy; but outside the camp he was confronted with the familiar racial segregation in public vehicles, and often with the flagrant disrespect of civilians for his status as a United States soldier in uniform.

It is only fair to point out, however, that although segregation of white and Negro troops has been general in the army, there have been notable exceptions. The authorities at Camp Lee, the largest quartermaster installation in the world, stressed interracial activities wherever consistent with military efficiency. To this end a mixed football team was placed in the field to represent the camp in competition with other camps. When this experiment was successful, interracial competition was sponsored in the sports program of the camp itself. This friendly rivalry developed mutual understanding and respect.

A policy of training selected groups of Negro and white soldiers together was also introduced. In the advanced quartermaster supply school, soldiers of both races were quartered together, and received instruction as a unit. The idea proved to be sound, and worth adoption elsewhere. One factor in the success of the plan was the soldiers selected for this kind of training. Some of them had college degrees, and all of them were chosen because they displayed qualities of individual initiative and a highly developed self-discipline.

An even more significant test was the use by the army of volunteer Negro platoons in several white infantry divisions during the final phases of the Ardennes counteroffensive and the Rhineland campaign. Men whom I talked with, both Negro and white, who fought in these mixed companies, agreed that the experiment was a success; and this seemed to be generally accepted throughout the army. At least one of the white divisions in which the test was made was predominantly from the deep South.

The results achieved by the army in these experiments confirmed the belief of many people that intelligent and mature individuals can get along under any circumstances. Negro soldiers who were chosen to take part in them welcomed the opportunity to mix with white soldiers on a basis of equality. They developed a self-assurance and a renewed faith in their abilities which destroyed any vestiges of cynicism or resentment which remained from their earlier experiences in the army.

The fact is that the Negro soldier has been anxious to do his part in this war, and has wanted that part to be an important contribution. He has resented above all the fact that he was usually assigned to labor units and service forces, since he shared the common belief that certain branches of the army are more important than others. Even when the equal importance of all branches of the armed forces in a chainlike dependency was pointed out to him, he did not always change his attitude. He would have preferred to take a more active part in the war, even though it meant greater risks to him. Indeed, his desire for self-esteem has been such, both for himself and for his race, that he has not hesitated to accept any dangers or responsibilities, even though they have involved giving his life for his country.

During the long period of time I was stationed at Camp Lee I had countless opportunities to watch the development of Negro youths, from raw recruits to trained soldiers and technicians. I was constantly impressed by the fact that the end result was for the better, so far as the individual was concerned. He was taught the importance of taking care of his body, his clothes, and his equipment. He formed a new conception of teamwork, in which the rating of his unit depended on the efforts of every soldier, and in which the laxness of one man could lower the standing of all. The result was that, contrary to what might have been expected, he became more conscious of his importance as an individual.

When the soldiers came from a rural Southern background, this sometimes created difficulties for their commanding officer. At the beginning of their basic training course, such men were unsure of themselves and greatly in awe of their officers. As their training progressed their attitude changed, and they often showed a temporary belligerency which sprang from their new sense of self-importance. The more efficient and intelligent commanding officers were able to direct this belligerency into constructive channels. The Negro soldier himself soon came to recognize that the maximum efficiency of his unit required the greatest possible use of all his talents and latent abilities. A man with a high-school education or a knowledge of some trade was more useful than an untutored one, and gained a prestige in the military community which was not obtainable by the untutored or the unskilled. This caused many Negro soldiers to clamor for admission to army trade schools, and to use every opportunity offered to obtain more formal education. It is to be hoped that the understanding they have gained of the advantages of special training will carry over into civilian life.

Despite the progress which individual Negroes have made, and despite more enlightened policies on the part of the army, the average Negro has felt that his abilities and talents were not utilized by the army to the best advantage. He has believed that too often his qualifications were lost by submergence in labor units and service forces, and that too much skilled Negro ability was dissipated in the maze of malassignment. While he has recognized that some malassignment is an inevitable part of the military picture, his awakened desire to prove his worth as an individual has made him more resentful of this state of affairs than the average white soldier.

But even the failure to appreciate his abilities has not affected the patriotism of the Negro soldier in so far as I have been able to observe in almost three years of army life. Whatever Japanese or German propaganda got through to him in the early years of the war fell upon fallow ground. Attempts to enlist the sympathies of the Negro on the side of Japan were rarely effective after Pearl Harbor; and before that they carried weight only among certain groups of discontented intellectuals. These men, when drafted, were soon reoriented by the morale program of the army.

The German government attempted to create friction among Negro soldiers on the battlefields of Europe. In Italy the Ninety-second Division was subjected to a barrage of German pamphlets. The leaflets which were dropped contained messages designed to create a nostalgia for home and a distrust of the white people of America. Soldiers were reminded that at home the Negro had to do all the dirty work. Surrender to enemy sentinels was advised, and fair treatment and comfortable housing in a modern, sanitary prison camp were promised, as well as an early return home after the war was over. Such propaganda had no effect.

But the morale of the Negro soldier, though relatively good, has been influenced by the activities of certain groups within his race who were anxious to take advantage of the present crisis to further the cause of the Negro in relation to white society. The intentions of such groups were of the best, and they were trying only to interpret the desires and hopes of the Negro to the American people. Unfortunately, what they had to say often increased the difficulties of the soldier in his adjustment to military life.

The constant barrage of agitation directed toward the soldier by the Negro press is an example of this kind of influence. Incidents of racial injustice were constantly played up so that the Negro soldier was reminded of his unequal status as a member of a minority group. Fortunately, the average soldier soon developed a self-restraint from his disciplined life in the army which curbed his desire to take action over a lynching in the South or a riot in a distant city. Even though he was not stirred to violence he did occasionally cherish a resentment which nullified to some extent the good effects of the army morale program.

As might have been expected, the general morale of the Negro soldiers with whom I was in close contact at Camp Lee varied from time to time. I remember one time when the officers who were charged with the maintenance of morale became worried at the growing discontent of the Negro troops and conceived of an intelligent and effective method of combating it. They gathered a number of news and army releases which praised the performance of Negro units and individual soldiers in the combat zones abroad. These exploits were presented to the soldiers and had a positive and immediate effect upon their state of mind. This was in interesting contrast to the attitude of the returning veterans themselves who had taken part in these exploits. They seemed to resent any special praise or attention given them because of their race.

I understood this attitude much better after I myself had been in Europe a few months. The numerous contacts which Negro troops in Europe have had with white civilians with little or no racial prejudice have had an undeniable effect on them, and will inevitably result in different attitudes after the war. The average Negro soldier landed in England, Africa, or Europe conscious of his color and ashamed, to a greater or lesser degree, of his dark skin. To his surprise, he was received by most civilians with wholehearted friendliness. In England, for example, he was impressed by the forthright approach of the British to the race problem which had been thrust upon them, and· he could not but admire their candid frankness in discussing it. In general, the Negro soldier in England tried to measure up to the standard of personal conduct and appearance which the British people seemed to expect of him; and as a result he was able to achieve a level of social contact with white civilians which had been denied him in his own country. A Negro soldier whom I met in France, and who had spent some time in England, told me an amusing story which had been going the rounds among British civilians. The young daughter of an English farmer was walking along a deserted country lane at nightfall when a truck loaded with Negro soldiers, and driven by a Negro, came up behind her. The sergeant in command of the detachment leapt down from the truck and asked her where she was going. She said that she was on her way home. He brusquely ordered her into the truck, which she mounted with fear and trembling, and he then demanded detailed directions to her home. When the truck reached it the sergeant helped her out and walked to the door with her. As her father appeared, the sergeant said to him, severely, "Don't you know that there is a camp of white Yankees just over the hill, and that it isn't safe for your daughter to be out alone at night?"

Such a story, whether apocryphal or not, seemed to me an interesting indication of the state of mind of the British people, which has certainly had its effect on the American Negroes who have come in contact with it. On the Continent the relationship between Negro soldiers and white civilians has been complicated by factors which did not exist in England. The liberated populations were hungry, and had just emerged from years of German oppression. The American troops, whether white or black, were hailed as liberators; and, partly through gratitude and partly as barter for food, many white women were ready to give themselves to the soldiers, regardless of color. It is difficult to foresee the effect of these contacts on the Negro troops who have taken advantage of them. The problem created is one which must be faced by the army and by the Americans in this country. Many Negro soldiers will return home with an attitude toward white women which may require a period of re-education if serious consequences are not to result. Most of all, the Negro soldier himself must face the situation realistically, and remember that the attitude of a liberated and hungry people is not to be confused with that of a more normal society to which he will return.

The dangers involved in the Negroes' experiences in liberated countries have been balanced by one distinct advantage. Many Negroes, including myself, were very much impressed by the degradation and poverty under which so many people in Europe are living today. We had never before seen white people living in conditions which would, in America, have placed them at the bottom of society. The result is that we have obtained a new perspective on our own country and on the advantages of the American way of life. We realize that, despite the disadvantages under which we live in America, we have much to be thankful for. As might have been expected, we take a new pride in our American citizenship, and realize for the first time its value in relation to the rest of the world.

I am now on board a transport of mixed troops bound from Europe to the Pacific. For the first few days we hoped that we were going home. When it was evident that we were headed East instead of West, white and Negro soldiers alike began to complain about the food, the showers, the heat, and the crowded conditions.

I was worried lest the ill temper of the soldiers result in interracial friction. All too often, in circumstances such as these, the Negro becomes a scapegoat on which the other fellow vents his spleen. But nothing of the sort happened. Instead, the soldiers on board seemed to become more considerate and tolerant of one another. I had been conscious that the Negro troops were watching for any signs of favoritism shown toward the whites, and it was a great relief to discover that the authorities in charge were enforcing the ship's regulations with complete impartiality. Both blacks and whites were subjected to the same inconveniences. If a latrine was occupied, a line formed without regard to color. In the distribution of the ship's paper, the individual soldier shared a copy with his neighbor, whoever it might be. The Negro troops, for whom the prospect of a work detail is omnipresent, were surprised when they learned that K.P. on board the ship was on a voluntary basis. As a reward, the soldier who volunteered was entitled to an extra meal a day.

The space on the ship for exercise and recreation was overcrowded at all times, and the soldiers were thrown together often literally as well as figuratively. Men stumbled over one another, bruising shins and turning ankles. A lurch of the ship would often put the foot of a passer-by in the middle of a poker game, but no hard feelings resulted, as each soldier realized that sooner or later he might be an offender. White soldiers joined Negro soldiers in card games, conversations, and the inevitable huddles in which veterans exchanged experiences and memories. They sat side by side in the movies. Negro soldiers naturally tended to associate with members of their own race, as did the whites, but I was interested to observe that in individual contacts of whites and Negroes the discussion was largely of their common stake in the war and in the peace to follow. I am convinced, from my own experiences in the armed forces both in the United States and in Europe, that a tolerance and understanding will exist between black and white veterans; and I hope it will have a definite effect on race relations in America. Many of the difficulties which arose in England between troops awaiting the invasion in Normandy, would hardly have occurred between veterans who had fought through Italy, France, Luxemburg, and Germany together.

The Negro soldier will return to civilian life with certain ambitions heightened by his army experience and with a greater desire to participate in society as a respected individual. He will be fully conscious of the contribution he has made to the winning of the war and will possess an inner assurance that he has earned the right to receive all the benefits that a grateful nation can give. Like his white comrade in arms, he must have the opportunity to serve as a useful member of society in the postwar world; and this opportunity must not be clouded by any makeshift expediencies or false fronts.

Many Negro soldiers have returned from active service overseas conscious of the fact that they have done a good job because they were good soldiers, trained and skilled in the techniques of warfare. The fact that they resent any special attention given to their accomplishments because they are Negroes, indicates, in my opinion, a new maturity on their part and augurs well for their postwar adjustment.

Many leaders in public life, particularly in the South where the rehabilitation problem of the Negro will be most urgent, are trying to lay the foundation now for a better society for the returning veteran. Realizing that he will be impatient of some phases of prewar race relations, if they still exist, such as segregation and housing shortages, they would like to improve these conditions before he returns. There is also in many states considerable agitation against the poll-tax laws, which affect six million white citizens as well.

Better housing for the Negro veterans is a must. They have traveled extensively while in army service and have seen the better homes of other Americans. They will not be satisfied with the prewar slum conditions still existing in many Negro urban areas. On the other hand, the housing accommodations constructed in industrial centers for war workers will not be acceptable to them, because they will recognize that these flimsy, makeshift structures are potential slums unless great sums of money are expended for their upkeep. Any attempt to foist them on the Negro veterans in lieu of modern housing units will meet with belligerent refusal.

It is probable that in the South the returning Negro veterans will seek housing facilities equal to those of the whites, rather than agitate for a change in segregation policies in residential areas. Any attempt by more radical Negro leaders to obtain unsegregated housing units may well alienate the veteran. His war experiences will have made him more than ever a realist, and a better home is the most urgent of his needs. It is not likely that any agitation which would jeopardize his acquiring better living conditions will receive his support. Moreover, many veterans will welcome the opportunity to prove to their white neighbors that they are capable of keeping their homes and neighborhoods up to the highest established standards. In this connection many United States housing experts have commented upon the Negro's pride in his new home after he has been granted the opportunity of living in a modern government housing project.

The North presents the opposite problem. Here the pattern of segregation is less pronounced and is to a certain extent on an economic and cultural basis in the urban and suburban areas. The veterans will return to civilian life so keenly alert to any attempt on the part of society to enforce racial discrimination that their leaders will refuse to accept better living quarters if such new arrangements are to be segregated. It was for this reason that a group of Negroes in Harlem recently succeeded in stopping a contemplated housing project which was sponsored by a large insurance company. It will be interesting to see what effect the return of the Negro veteran will have on this particular aspect of race relations.

There are indications that Negro veterans will achieve more tangible benefits in the South, because of an awakened spirit of cooperation on the part of Southern whites, and because of the more conservative policies of Negro leaders. Here the veterans will return to a more established and more integrated Negro society. Their army life has not greatly disturbed the normal pattern of their segregated social life. They have, however, been influenced to some extent by contacts with Negro soldiers from the North and with unprejudiced white civilians abroad, and have felt the urge existing in their comrades, both white and black, to make this a better world after the war.

While they may not seriously object to segregation in

housing, they will certainly be much less willing than before to accept segregation in public vehicles and in public places.

Fortunately, enlightened Southern leaders are keenly aware of the danger of attempting to gain their ends by legislative means in a society where prejudice is still rampant, and where the franchise for Negroes is still largely restricted. They realize that laws against human prejudice are more easily made than enforced, and that often the tension created when such laws are passed increases rather than diminishes prejudice. Until the Negro is in a position to cast his vote, and therefore become a power in the political life of his community, it is better that he work through the tried and tested means of liberal interracial groups and gradual education of the community, rather than through legislative measures or the courts.

The South is in many ways more provincial than the North, particularly in agricultural sections. It is not uncommon to hear a citizen of a southern state refer to one of another as a "foreigner." In view of this strong community feeling, many leaders feel that the more immediate racial problems can best be solved on a local basis, and that attempts to achieve too many reforms through government action may serve only to increase racial tension.

The Southern Negro soldier has become more conscious than ever of his rights and privileges as a citizen of a democracy. His contacts with Northern Negroes and his army training have increased considerably his interest in the ballot. While millions of Negroes, through discriminatory poll-tax laws or Democratic party regulations, have been kept from exercising their right to vote, almost as many have made little or no effort to use their franchise where it was available to them.

Dr. Luther P. Jackson of Virginia State College for Negroes at Ettrick, Virginia, has carefully studied the franchise situation as it applies to the Negro in his native state. He has found that 366,717 Negroes in Virginia were of voting age, but that of this number only 9 per cent had met the poll-tax requirements.

In order to vote in Virginia, a citizen must have paid his poll-tax for the three preceding years. While 80,000 Negroes in 1943 had paid at least a part of their poll tax for the necessary three years only 32,504 had paid in full; and 40 per cent of these failed to register. Racial discrimination as such did not prevent them from doing so, since most registrars recognize no color line. Undoubtedly, most of the Negroes who failed to keep up their poll-tax payments were, under war conditions, financially able to do so; and their failure to qualify as voters represented a self-imposed disenfranchisement.

Dr. Jackson in no sense defends the poll tax, but he does draw critical attention to the fact that the great majority of Negroes could and should be more alert in exercising their right to vote. Despite his disappointments in the past, and the lack of effectiveness of his vote in solving the problems which confront him, the Negro should certainly make a greater effort to fulfill this important obligation of a good citizen.

The returning Negro veterans in the South who have been made conscious of the ballot and its potential importance to

them will still need careful preparation for the exercise of
their franchise. As the right to vote is gradually extended to
them in the more backward southern states, such acts might
well carry a provision for the setting up of advisory committees which could orient and instruct the veterans as to
their new rights and obligations. Just as the Negro has been
taught many skills and aptitudes in the army which have
made it possible for him to give his utmost to the war effort,
so, as a citizen, he should be taught how he can best aid in
winning the peace.

Most important of all for the returning veteran will be
the question of a job. In an article published in April, 1945,
Julius A. Thomas, director of the Department of Industrial
Relations of the National Urban League, presented an interesting and informative survey of the occupational status of
Negro workers during the war. He points out that at that
time more than 1,500,000 Negro workers were employed in
industrial plants producing essential war material. He also
shows that despite this remarkable record, which has been
duplicated at no other time in our history, Negro men were
still largely employed as farmers, farm laborers and general
laborers, the women in domestic and personal service occupations. This pattern of employment has changed little since
the days of slavery. The progress which Negro workers have
made in obtaining and holding jobs as skilled industrial
workers has not been uniform in different sections of the
country, nor has it included all industries. However, a recently completed survey of the performance of Negro workers in three hundred war plants shows that in two hundred
and fifty of these nearly 100,000 Negro workers were em-

ployed, approximately half of them as skilled or semi-skilled workers. Furthermore, the managers of the vast majority of plants agree that they are doing an acceptable job. This, in many cases, is due to the active and intelligent guidance which the Urban League has given to Negro workers in adjusting themselves to the regularity and tempo of industrial employment. Only three out of the three hundred plants included in the survey segregated Negro and white workers; and in these three plants segregation applied only to Negro skilled workers and machine operators. Only six plants— and these were located in the South—reported separate eating and comfort facilities.

It is perhaps too early to foresee the future of these wartime workers, to say nothing of the million Negro men and women who have been serving in the Armed Forces; but the early postwar period will see a larger number of Negroes than ever before with new skills and abilities, either in civilian life or in the army, who want to employ these skills to the best advantage. Mr. Thomas ends his article with the statement that this is a problem with which vocational counselors, educators, employers, social workers, labor leaders, government officials, and the public must inevitably come to grips.

For the returning veteran, it will be not a theoretical but a practical problem, and one which he will have to face as soon as he is mustered out. I have talked with many Negro soldiers and questioned them about their postwar plans. Many do not want to return to their old type of employment, because their army life has opened up new vistas to them and released unsuspected abilities. One soldier said that he was going into business for himself because he no longer wanted to work for anybody, even if he had to sell shoestrings. This veteran was determined to have greater independence, but he represents, I think, the exception. Many returning veterans, through force of circumstances, will inevitably drift back into the type of work which they were doing before the war; but they will be far from content if they are not permitted to use some, at least, of the skills which they have acquired in the army. The period of demobilization might well be used by the army to reorient colored soldiers to the postwar world. It is yet too early to foresee how many Negroes can be absorbed by industry in the postwar period; and much might be done before the men are released, to prepare them for a possible situation in which they will be forced back into service employment. I do not mean to imply, however, that every means should not be used by an enlightened democracy to break down the prejudices still existing in industry and to increase as rapidly as possible the opportunities open to skilled Negro workers.

The average veteran will have witnessed, during his service in the army, a gradual liberalizing of the War Department's policies in reference to him as a Negro. He will return to civilian life with a greater self-respect as a Negro and as a human being, which will help him to face with tolerance and courage the problems which will again confront him when he is out of uniform. He will possess a greater sense of realism than ever before, and a conviction that he has earned certain tangible rewards from society which have not heretofore been accorded him.

The so-called G. I. Bill of Rights, if applied without discrimination, will be of definite assistance to him in the early postwar era. It is important that the Negro veteran, even more than his white comrade, be fully informed of all the benefits and opportunities accorded to him under the provisions of this law. If properly applied it can give him the opportunity to acquire the academic and technical education which he needs and desires, and which alone can assure him of ultimate security.

In the war the Negro soldier has come face to face with the knowledge that any way of life to survive must have adherents who are willing to die for it. He will have realized that this extreme devotion to a way of life exists both in his own ranks and in those of the enemy. He himself will have been fighting for democracy, and for a democracy that has in some measure withheld from him as a Negro privileges and advantages which others of his fellow citizens enjoy. Through his active participation in this struggle to defend America, he has for the first time realized how much a part of America he is, and he is beginning to think in terms of what he can do, individually and collectively, to make his country a better place to live in for himself and his children.

With the prestige which he will have on his return among the members of his own race, it is essential that this new spirit be used as a cornerstone for the building of a better democracy for whites and blacks alike. If it is allowed to be dissipated, as it can easily be, by the tensions and humiliations which he suffered in the prewar world, the cause of better racial relations may be set back a generation.

★ 7 ★

The Negro and Democracy

THE Negroes of America still believe in democracy and are believing more and more that they have something to offer to this way of life. Their patience and loyal solicitude for those they serve are qualities akin to that brotherhood which fits men best for democracy; and this solicitude is not easily diverted. In the home of a well-to-do America politician a Negro girl was employed to do the housework and take charge of the children. Her duties and responsibilities were many, and her wages were considerably less than the prevailing level. Overworked, and with better opportunities available, she constantly told her friends of her intention to leave; but strangely she made no move to do so. In explanation, she finally confessed, "If I did, who would look after the house and the children the way I do?"

This tradition of loyalty has a long history. The forefathers of the present-day Negro-American were torn from a society in which loyalty was due to one man as the head of the tribe. In America they were sold to masters who expected and got both work and obedience from them often, it is true, by means of the whip; but in many instances humane masters received in return for their kindness the devoted loyalty of their slaves. Indeed, during the Civil War, there was a superlative exhibition by many Negroes of loyalty and chivalry toward defenseless women and children such as has seldom been excelled in the annals of man.

The habit of giving of himself is very strong in the Negro; but it has for too long been a one-sided giving. Now, at last, he is beginning to be aware of how small the returns have been and to realize that he is needed and has the possibility of being appreciated. The Negro no longer feels that there is nothing for him to do but stand idly by while others build new and better worlds. Whether his rights as a citizen have been recognized or not, he is beginning to feel that his own future is a part of the destiny of America, to which he himself will have something to contribute.

The Negro's consciousness of belonging to America has persisted despite the many attempts by white Americans to make him feel out of place. Many times in segregated sections of public places Negroes have stood in respectful attention when the national anthem was played. While conscious on such occasions of their segregation, few Negroes can suppress a deep surge of emotional patriotism which rises above any sense of injustice and bitterness. This feeling of devotion to his country is a part of his American heritage. It has been tested by two hundred fifty years of ceaseless slave labor and almost a century more of economic slavery.

Patience, which is democracy's way, is natural to the Negro. Despite a deep sense of frustration he has, from the beginning, shunned violence as a means of obtaining the social and economic security he so profoundly desires. This respect for the democratic way has often been misinterpreted.

The Negro's tolerance and his faith in America have sometimes been construed as cowardice; but actually he has heretofore rejected violence as a means of obtaining his ends because he has instinctively realized the futility of force where good relations are sought.

The Negro understands another truth forgotten by many Americans. It is that faith in religious principles and their everyday application is far more important than man-made concepts of law and order. Negro slaves withstood the brutality of slavery by holding fast to their faith in God. They learned that Christianity was the one force strong enough to support them under the yoke of their owners. The right to worship God was a privilege that could not be taken away from the Negroes. Under the lash of the whip they could still murmur, "God have mercy."

In the early days in this country slaves were in some instances forbidden to worship. Quietly in the middle of the night they would gather in one of the plantation shacks to commune with God. Softly they would pray. Silently a religious fervor would come over the gathering. For they dared not raise their voices, and the fear of the master's whip would still their desire to release in a wild torrent of sound the deep spiritual emotion they felt. Many of them would shake with emotion, and soon the shack would be filled with hushed, swaying slaves who could not be kept from their one solace, worship of God.

The Negro learned that earthly pain could be lost in the glory of worshiping God. He grew to trust his faith and the word of God. His suffering often became for him a period of spiritual growth. The knowledge that God was more important than any other single force in the existence of mankind gave hope and power to his dream of a better world on earth. Eventually, when the Negro came to know more about democracy, he recognized it for what it was—a way of life founded on principles similar to those of a faith he had already learned to cherish.

The Negro has had few benefits from American democracy, and these often at a high cost; but he retains his faith in it. He knows instinctively that one of the basic requirements of good citizenship in a democracy is the ability to live and work in harmony with all kinds of people, and this is something at which he excels. Most Negroes, when they wish to use it, have a simple, direct way of establishing a bond of communication with those whom they meet. Their ability to win friends in high and low places has been a most important factor in their fight to survive and to win a place for themselves in American life. In fact the Negro possesses a natural sense of sound values in human relationships.

Perhaps this is explained by the fact that the true Negro lacks both the snobbishness and the acquisitiveness which are so characteristic of much of Occidental society. In proportion to their earnings, Negroes are the greatest spenders in the world. The spectacle of a decrepit old man worrying himself into a nervous collapse because he fears that a war or depression will destroy his business or his investments brings gales of laughter to any group of Negroes. To hoard up goods for tomorrow is an aim alien to Negro thought.

A white man said to a group of Negroes recently, "You people seem to get along on so little, and still you are happy."

"Yes," replied one of them, "a little, and the right to enjoy that little, is all we want."

Perhaps more than any other group in the United States, the Negroes are aware that the Four Freedoms cannot be achieved without four sacrifices by those members of society who have denied them these freedoms in the past. Freedom from Want implies the abandonment by more favored groups of greed and exploitation. Freedom from Fear can be his only if others give up persecuting him. Freedom of Religion will be a hollow mockery if those who worship the same God deny him a place at their altars. Freedom of Speech only adds to his burdens if it is used by prejudiced demagogues to revile and belittle him.

Twice within the twentieth century America has rallied all her forces to fight for her democratic ideals. If this war too is not to have been fought in vain, America must assume world leadership in the cause of democracy. And democracy, if it is to be real and worth fighting for, must be more than an ideal or a theory. It must become a way of life for all its citizens.

Others besides myself have pointed out the inconsistency of a government and a people in fighting abroad for a way of life which they are unable or unwilling to apply to a sizable proportion of their own citizens. In the last analysis, our government is a government of the people; and until the people themselves—meaning you and me—are willing to accept a tolerant and understanding attitude toward one another, we shall be weak where we should be strongest; namely, on the home front.

Tolerance follows understanding, and understanding comes most easily through rubbing elbows as co-workers, neighbors, acquaintances, and friends. One of the first steps toward this end is the acceptance by whites of Negroes in public places. Many persons of intelligence but of limited comprehension of the Negro point of view, or indeed of themselves, have been known to say that the Negro hurts his own cause by insisting upon being accepted in such semipublic places as good hotels and shops. Unless a man can bring himself to the point of being undisturbed by the presence of a person of color at a neighboring table in a restaurant, and unless his wife can face with equanimity the presence of other shoppers of a darker hue in her favorite department store, they will be a long way from taking one of the simplest and easiest steps in racial tolerance.

There is, and should be, no law which compels any of us to accept as acquaintances or friends individuals of whom we disapprove. If such discrimination on our part is made on the basis of character and community of interest, we are only exerting one of the primary privileges of a democratic way of life. If, however, color is the determining factor— regardless of the other qualifications which an individual may bring to such an acquaintanceship—not only is the cultural and community life of both whites and blacks limited, but there exists little opportunity for either race to gain greater understanding of the other.

This intolerance on the part of too large a proportion of white Americans is matched by an attitude on the part of many Negroes which is equally censurable, and just as dangerous to the cause of better race relations. This is the attitude of aggression mixed with defiance, which some Negroes display in public places. The basis of this attitude is often a reflection of the scorn and disapproval which they sense around them; even where these are only imagined, it is an instinctive protest against past indignities, expressing itself through some of the less pleasant workings of a defense psychology.

It is this whole vicious circle which must be broken down, and the Negro should not hesitate to take the first step. Important as it is to the white race and to the future of democracy in the United States that white America develop a tolerant attitude toward the Negro, it is of even greater importance to the Negro. Therefore, as the realist that he is, he should recognize to the fullest his own responsibilities in the matter and should train himself to give up the momentary satisfaction of expressing his age-old resentment for the sake of a greater ultimate reward.

It would be very fortunate for all of us if I or anyone else could conceive of a single means of bringing to pass a new era of race relations in the United States. I know of none, nor do I know of anyone who does. Many worthy attempts have been and are being made by groups and individuals, some of which I have already mentioned. Except in those instances where the problem of Negro-white relationship is used by interested groups to further a program which to most of us seems un-American, all these efforts are to be commended. In view of the long-standing existence of the problem, due in my opinion in this country to a carry-over from the master-slave relationship, it is one which cannot be solved by any easy panacea. The combined efforts of all of us working through every means at hand come finally to the ultimate stumbling block of the individual. All of us without exception must learn to accept one another as members of one race, the human race. We must educate ourselves to the point where the color of a man's skin is of no more importance than the color of his eyes, and where our evaluations of one another are on the basis of character and interests rather than on creed or color.

Such education can come only with time; but unfortunately we cannot tell how much time we have. We know that unless a working solution of the race problem in this country can be achieved soon, now that the war is over, we shall be in danger of a calamity which might have as devastating an effect on the nation as the continuance of the war itself. It might have an even more devastating effect if our inability to solve our domestic problems in a democratic way should cause the whole theory of democracy to lose caste in the eyes of the world.

And if America is unwilling or unable to make its own democratic way of life the forerunner of a new cultural influence in the life of all mankind our youth, both black and white, will have died in vain.